CU00900965

Edinburgh in the Shadows

Stories, tales and poems from the Fringe show
written and performed by
Alec Beattie and Max Scratchmann
with illustrations by
Gracia Navas

ISBN 978-1530760411

Edinburgh in the Shadows
is published by
Shadows Publishing

edinburghintheshadows.wordpress.com

Edinburgh
in the
Shadows

[signatures]

Shadows Publishing

Contents

Fancy Some Inhaling?

Alec Beattie

James Young Simpson, the Edinburgh obstetrician who pioneered the use of chloroform as an anaesthetic, is reputed to have held after-dinner drug parties where he would encourage his guests to inhale handkerchiefs he had soaked with various different liquid chemicals so he could observe the effects. After years of experimenting on himself his health had begun to deteriorate so he passed on the responsibility of inhaling the contents of decanters he kept in his study to his family and friends, all in his quest to find a substance that would render the recipient unconscious and insensitive to pain. On the 4th of November 1847 he held one such party where Simpson and two of his colleagues literally stumbled upon the anaesthetic properties of chloroform. Also present that night were his wife Jessie, and his niece Adelia Petrie who recorded the events in her diary...

Fancy some inhaling...?

From the diary of Miss Adelia Petrie, 5th November 1847:

I went to my Auntie Jessie's and Uncle Jim's last night for my dinner. Uncle Jim's pals from work Duncan and Keith were there as well. After dinner Uncle Jims says will you ladies excuse us three gentlemen - we fancy some inhaling, and Duncan says to me that they've been doing it for weeks now, inhaling chemicals and stuff to see what the effects are.

Aye, says Keith. All in the interest and advancement of science.

Would you ladies care to observe, says Uncle Jim, and we all piled into his study.

Inside the room there's a huge sideboard with all these decanters lined up along the top. Duncan goes and picks one up and hands it to me. Miss Petrie, Duncan says, would you care to inhale some of this?

Oh, I says, I don't know...

Come now, Miss Petrie, says Keith. All in the interest and advancement of science.

I guarantee, Miss Petrie, says Duncan, that the effects are rather amusing.

I take the top off and have a big sniff at the decanter. After a bit I says, nothing's happening. What's this stuff anyway?

Then Duncan bursts out laughing and says, that's my piss you're sniffing. Everyone else starts laughing and even though I was mad as anything I had to just sit there and take it! Then Uncle Jim says right, gentlemen! You can stop taking the piss out of my niece! And then he lets another wee laugh. Now - to work! He picks up another decanter and says, this came this morning, all the way from Germany.

It's called chloroform. Go on, Duncan, and Uncle Jim takes the top off the decanter and holds it under Duncan's nose. He takes a big man-sniff then the next thing he's on the floor!

Everyone goes all quiet as if Duncan's died or something, and then it hits me - I should have thrown Duncan's piss in his face but I missed my chance so instead I stand up and go over and kick Duncan right in the groin but all he does is groan a wee bit and open his eyes.

Did I just pass out? He says.

Astounding, Uncle Jim says, excited. Tell me Duncan, quickly now, are you experiencing any pain?

No, says Duncan. Should I be?

No pain, eh? Says Uncle Jim, looking at the decanter of chloroform. Keith! Do the honours, please.

Then Keith comes over and has a big sniff as well and then he's on the floor, snoring away. I ask Uncle Jim if I should give Keith a boot in the groin as well. All for the interest and advancement of science.

No need, says Uncle Jim, and he hands the decanter to me, takes a big snort and then slumps to the floor, taking a header into Auntie Jessie's good coffee table on the way down.

Jesus wept, says Auntie Jessie. Call yourself scientists? Any idiot would sit down first before huffing on that stuff.

After a while, when the men have recovered and finished boasting about who's inhaled the most chloroform, Uncle Jim says to me that I should try it as well.

For the interest and advancement of society, says Duncan, but I'm not keen on hanging about with three old guys getting off their heads on God-knows-what so I make my excuses and head on home.

4

When I rose this morning there was a message from Auntie Jessie waiting for me. It said that I should come for dinner again this evening and that everyone was inhaling something they'd discovered after I'd left the previous evening, something called methylenedioxymethamphetamine. She also said she was rolling balls. Well, dear Diary, I'm still not too keen on inhaling any of Uncle Jim's chemicals but I must say I'm very much looking forward to a few games of carpet bowls with my Auntie Jessie.

Houdini's Foot Fetish

Max Scratchmann

There are loads of stories about Harry Houdini, the legendary magician and escapologist, but what most people don't realise is that this Wisconsin lad was very much a part and parcel of Edinburgh life, performing both in the city and Leith many, many times over the years, and he frequently packed out the Empire Palace (now the big glass-fronted Festival Theatre) as well as the Gaiety on the waterfront. (Seems that most Leithers wouldn't make the epic journey into Auld Reekie to see him!)

But there's one particular story about Edinburgh's favourite rabbi's son that I want to share with you today. Houdini had been making Scottish headlines in the bitter winter of 1912 when he'd promised to be chained up and thrown into the – no doubt – tropical waters of Aberdeen harbour in the middle of a severe gale, and it was only when the local coast guard assured him in their flat Doric tones that "naebuddy" was going to go out to rescue his mad American ass if the stunt went wrong that he finally agreed to be thrown into the breakwater of the Navigation Channel instead. Though the water there was so full of untreated sewage that it's a wonder that he didn't instantly poison himself when he disappeared below the waves wrapped in all his hardware.

It was his next stunt, however, that got Edinburgh

talking, when, undeterred by his winter dip in the North Sea he came down to the capital and started a new sensation by announcing in the press that he was "horrified" by the number of barefoot children in the streets and would personally provide a good pair of boots to any child presenting himself at the theatre in Nicholson Street.

Unsurprisingly, the City's street urchins quickly smelled loot, and word spread like wildfire, as Houdini knew it would, and there was no doubt more than one child who stashed his own boots and then went out to get a gratis new pair courtesy of the city's favourite visitor. Kids lined the street leading to the theatre for hours, and though Houdini had stockpiled five hundred pairs of boots for the stunt they had soon all been distributed, and so, in a bizarre procession like a northern version of the Pied Piper of Hamelin, he took a long crocodile of waifs and strays out to a local cobbler's and had them all shod while he waited.

And, whatever Houdini's motives – philanthropic or mercenary – it can't be denied that the man loved to rise to a challenge, and he was always pushing people to invent some new contraption that he couldn't get out of, sweetening the deal with the offer of a hundred pounds for that elusive inescapable box, and the punters flocked to the theatres in their droves to see him wriggle his way out of the latest reinforced-concrete iron maiden that Wee Shuggie from Piershill had devised.

"Houdini has accepted a challenge from four employees of Mr Adam Currie, Building Contractor, Newington Works, Edinburgh, to escape from a strongbox," one advert for the Empire in 1914 read. "Constructed in full view of the audience, the lid will be nailed down, and the box roped up" and – according to eye witnesses – three "expert" joiners from Leith then secured the specially constructed box and sat back with the rest of the audience to await Houdini's appearance while the rich velvet curtains came down in front of the casket.

According to the Scotsman review: "It was almost twelve minutes before the drapery in front of the pavilion was swept aside and Houdini appeared, showing the box apparently intact and in the same condition as before he entered it. He said jocularly, the only difference was that whereas before he was inside, now he was outside."

Unsurprisingly, no-one ever managed to win Houdini's hundred pounds – though I suspect that more than a few fivers changed hands back stage for all those trapdoors that were secreted in the boxes, but what I really wonder about in the dark hours when I can't sleep, is what did the audience do for the twelve minutes or so that it took Houdini to escape – talk amongst themselves?

chained up

Houdini's Visit to Edinburgh

Max Scratchmann

He suffocates in a symphony of steel,
Clanking chains hewn from a
Mixed hardware of sieves and garden rakes
Smelted down into his self-inflicted bondage weave,
More terrible than the icy waters of the Forth,
As the clank-clank-clank of cogged wheels
Lower him down to the murky depths.

Hell, wasn't this supposed to be Lock Ness?

But the monsters are firmly in his own head
And he comes supplied with his very own batch of
Personal demons,
Fork-tailed and razor-sharp,
Perambulating openly with him
In the ticker-tape parade on the Royal Mile,
Then taking-in an excursion of Princes Street escapology
In the grand hall of Jenners,
Before being thrown,
Cocooned in ropes and weights,
From the pin-sharp pinnacles of the Scott Monument,
Disappointing the cheering crowd
Who have gathered to see him die
In the middle of the gardens,
A howling aria of fauna, blood and bone.

But, no, Houdini thwarts the malevolent ectoplasm
Of his dead mother and lands
Triumphant
On angels wings of riveted steel and goose feathers.

And the Edinburgh-rock-crunching crowd boos as they disperse,
Vexed that there is to be no blood today,
But, as Houdini takes his final bow,
He winks a promise,
For he never disappoints,
There *will* be blood and death,
Just,
Not yet.

My Own Havoc

Alec Beattie

In 1997 a badly burned, handwritten manuscript was found in the National Library of Scotland and was quickly verified as belonging to Robert Louis Stevenson. This gave credence to the claim made by Stevenson's wife that she made him destroy the original version of 'Jekyll and Hyde'; she complained it 'said much that it should not,' and that its publication would ruin Stevenson. In the version of the novel we all know, Jekyll believing he would become Hyde permanently and be punished for Hyde's crimes, took his own life. In the original version, he does not; he transforms into Hyde and suddenly disappears...

Throughout the years following my final and irreversible transformation I have been very careful to conceal my identity. Although outwardly I have retained the features of Edward Hyde, I have done all I can to conceal that fact; I have grown a full beard and have taken to wearing spectacles; I maintain an upright posture and walk slowly and carefully; and I have moved from that part of London where I would be more readily recognised by my - and Jekyll's - former friends. Now I live quietly and comfortably in a more modest part of the city where I am sure I will remain safe from detection.

It is, however, much more difficult to conceal that part of myself that remains animalistic; even though I wrestle with that tiniest part of my conscience, the last scrap of the educated and civilised Jekyll, I am still driven to carry out barbaric acts. However, I must confess that in the five years of my remaining Hyde, I have learned to temper myself, to control that part of me that wants to lash out and beat without any thought. I have learned to be careful, methodical, and that I do not require either lashing out or beating; one might say that nowadays I am thoroughly clinical. I have also learned to avoid detection, and by this I mean capture by the Metropolitan Police.

For you see, I now know I was foolish in my most public act of killing Danvers Carew. I did not see this at the time; while I battered and beat him to death him I was overcome with a visceral delight that clouded out any degree of decent judgement I might have had. This is the reason I have removed myself to London's east end. Not one of Jekyll's acquaintances would lower himself to come here. Not even for the cheap and plentiful entertainment.

And when I learned that the police - hampered by their

limited use and constrained by their inflexible routines - relied on their presence alone to maintain peace and restrict lawlessness, I saw my opportunity: why not let Hyde wreak his own kind of havoc among the people of Whitechapel? As long as I remembered to temper myself, I knew my detection would be nigh on impossible, and my capture completely unfeasible.

At first I was anxious that I should be quick; my overwhelming concern was that I should not be caught in the act. Then I learned if I chose carefully I could afford to take a little more time, and with that I decided that, in order to maintain the thrill of it all, I should take a souvenir.
But now the newspapers are cashing in on my work. Daily they publish sensational stories of gore and horror that not only delight those who read newspapers; it also provokes people into believing they are me! They have even given me a name!

As I draw this period of my life to a conclusion (I am off soon to new shores and a New World) I feel I must point out to those who seek to imitate me that I was born, raised and educated in Edinburgh, and that I am no Jack. It would not do to give the police even the slightest clue as to my identity; suffice to say that, all things being equal, I would rather be referred to as *Jock* the Ripper.

Witchcraft in Edinburgh

Alec Beattie

Edinburgh certainly has a dark history filled with murder, executions, ghosts, hauntings, witches and grave robbers, to name but a few. Today the city utilises its past - mostly for the benefit of tourists who can go on ghost tours, visit execution sites or drink in the same taverns frequented by the murderers and resurrection men. It's all a bit fanciful and geared more towards the sensational rather than the factual. What follows is an attempt to redress the balance and offer the reader an account of witchcraft in Edinburgh, based more on historical fact...

Introduction

Medieval Scotland believed in fairies and devils as much as it believed in saints and angels. And, just as people readily accepted that priests had the power to forgive sins and change wine into Christ's blood, they believed that witches had the power to inflict curses or heal the sick. It was two sides of the same coin, a world of good and evil spirits where religious and folk beliefs existed in tandem and were tolerated, practiced, and deeply ingrained in all Scots at all levels of society.

However, the Protestant Reformation during the sixteenth century profoundly changed this. On the one hand, many aspects of Catholic worship were banned, or at the very least, suppressed. Celebrating the Mass, selling indulgences, and the use of relics, rituals and iconography were now regarded as idolatrous popery and heretical superstitions, and the people of Scotland began to worship in the way the Calvinist Scottish Kirk wanted them – belief in predestination and God's elect, the literal interpretation of the Bible, eternal damnation, the Kingdom of God here on earth. Nevertheless, the practice of traditional folk beliefs continued; people still sought herbal and plant remedies from so-called 'Guid Folk', visited magical places, and celebrated seasonal festivals.

However, a belief had begun to emerge in Europe that made its way to Scotland in the same way the Reformation had, and which gradually made witchcraft intolerable: there was a universal conspiracy by the Devil and his witches who were seeking to work against man and God. Now it was obvious to all correct-thinking people, regardless of their religious or political affiliations, that witches had to be extirpated. Furthermore, the widely-held belief that a distinction could be made between good and evil witches, those that cursed and those that cured, disappeared; all witches were to be persecuted. God made no exception in favour of the good witch.

The Scottish Witchcraft Act was introduced in 1563, and made witchcraft and conspiring with witches capital offenses. While the Act mentioned diabolical deeds such as witchcraft, sorcery, and necromancy, it never described what these actually were. As a consequence, together with many other factors, while the Act was in force until 1736, about 4000 people were tried in Scotland for witchcraft. The number who were executed may be as high as 3200. Although witchcraft was a criminal offense in statute law, the Scottish Presbyterian Kirk began to involve itself in the prosecution of those accused of witchcraft. The Kirk had managed to have witchcraft recognised as a special crime which meant that the normal rules of prosecution didn't apply; the use of torture to gain confessions and testimony from women and children was accepted. All acts of witchcraft were referred to as 'maleficium', acts designed to cause harm, the power to do so coming directly from the Devil.

To enter into a demonic pact (i.e. a pact with the Devil) a witch would have to forsake their Christian beliefs and promise themselves to the Devil in return for some earthly gifts or powers. This could take many different forms, from individual pacts to pacts made as a part of a group or Sabbat. The use of special devices, words and rituals would also be involved.

The perceptions of what witchcraft was fell into several categories, all regarded as maleficium: curses, spells, sorcery (which was the intended harm or death of people or property), healing, fortune telling, association with a reputed witch.

Continued use of the above, whether real or imagined ('white' magic, for example, the use of herbs and medicines), would lead to someone having the reputation of being a witch which in turn, depending on circumstances, would lead to an accusation of witchcraft.

In Scotland witch hunts or witch scares saw sharp increases in the number of people being accused of witchcraft, and usually occurred in tandem with other negative events such as poor weather and harvests, and war and political upheaval. Nevertheless, witchcraft practices went on; people such as midwives or those involved in medicine, for example, relied on their knowledge and skills to make a living, although most lived with the prospect of being denounced for witchcraft.

As witchcraft was prohibited by law, there was a legal process for the prosecution of witches.

Once a person had a reputation for being a witch, accusations of the use of witchcraft could soon follow, perhaps as a consequence of a quarrel with a neighbour; cursing and naming someone as a witch was no longer regarded as simple name calling. However, someone with a reputation would find accusations of witchcraft being taken far more seriously. Evidence would be gathered (and, as previously mentioned, witchcraft was seen as a special crime; testimony from women and children would be taken seriously). The accused would then be called before a Kirk session where a more formal investigation would be instigated. If there was a reasonable case to be answered the accused would then be arrested.

Evidence usually came from four different sources. Testimony from neighbours usually described arguments and quarrels with the suspect, typically following misfortunes suffered, such as an illness or the death of livestock. Testimony was taken from other witches who were also under suspicion during a trial as this was seen as an effective way of increasing the number of suspects during a trial and often occurred during intense spells of witch hunting. If the accused was not forthcoming with a confession then torture could be used. In Scotland sleep deprivation was widely employed. The accused would be kept awake for days on end, inducing susceptibility and hallucinations (which may account for some of the more overly-florid confessions gained in this way). Other forms of torture were used too, such as thumbscrews, the boot, and the branks. Finally the accused could be pricked to find the Devil's mark, given to a witch as part of their demonic pact. Typically this involved the accused being searched and insensitive parts of their body pricked with pins, usually blemishes and moles that didn't bleed.

The accused would then be tried at a secular court; despite its involvement in the prosecution of witches the Kirk did not have the power to execute anyone. The majority of witches in Scotland were tried in local courts that had been commissioned to carry out the trial. Witches found guilty of any crimes – whether it was an act prohibited by the Witchcraft Act, or for making a pact with the Devil, or for acts of maleficium – were condemned to death. Death usually meant strangulation at the stake, and the body was then burned.

Major Thomas Weir

It would seem strange for anyone accused of witchcraft – and perhaps knowing that their confession had been as a result of torture, or much likely, that they were innocent of any crimes - that they would freely admit to any guilt. Anyone, as seen above, found guilty would face a certain and grisly death. Many, at the point of their execution, would refuse to confess to any acts of witchcraft as they didn't want the sin of lying on their soul. But there are cases where people admitted at will to acts of witchcraft in full knowledge of their fate, such as Margaret Duchill who lived in Alloa in the 1650s.

Accused of witchcraft and arrested, she was subsequently questioned before confessing to the following: having made a pact with the Devil, having the power of flight, the ability to kill by her touch alone, both men and beasts, fornicating with demons, dancing and singing in Satan's honour, the power of foresight, casting spells…Margaret Duchill wasn't executed for her crimes; her trial record ends abruptly suggesting she died in custody.

Perhaps a better known story that's become part of Edinburgh lore is that of Major Thomas Weir. He was a lieutenant in the Scottish Covenanter army that fought alongside Cromwell during the Civil Wars, and captain of the Edinburgh guard in the 1650s. A religious zealot, he was regarded as a preacher of some repute and a man of some considerable standing. However, when he reached the age of 70 he fell ill and was nursed by his sister Jean who lodged with him in Edinburgh's West Bow. It was during this time that he freely admitted to witchcraft and having made a pact with the Devil. He also confessed to bestiality and incest, claims his sister readily affirmed as she was complicit in all these acts. The town's Lord Provost refused to believe them but when they insisted on having lived a life of debauchery and witchcraft, they were arrested. Weir was examined by a series of doctors as it was feared that the illness had affected his wits but all who inspected him pronounced him sane. While in custody Jean began to lose her wits and her confessions became ever more bizarre; Weir maintained that he was a warlock and sorcerer, and that he had lain with his sister on many occasions. Both were condemned; however, as he had been widely regarded as a highly-spiritual man, Weir was to be executed for the crimes of bestiality and incest while the charges of witchcraft were dropped.

Weir refused to ask for forgiveness, his final words being, 'I have lived as a beast, and I must die as a beast'. He was strangled and his body burned. His sister, her mental state much deteriorated, was hanged, but not before she managed to strip herself of her clothes and curse the watching crowd.

Soon after, stories began to circulate Edinburgh concerning Weir. Many people claimed to have seen him, a once-familiar figure in his long, black cloak and hat with his staff clearing a path for him, of its own volition, leading to claims that the staff acted as Weir's servant. The house they inhabited lay empty for decades before burning down; no-one could bring themself to live there and no-one could be induced to spend more than one night there. Stories of the house being haunted by various animals circulated, the most infamous being an unearthly calf. And many people claimed that, at midnight on certain nights of the year, a huge, fiery carriage, drawn by black horses, would come tearing down the West Bow, carrying Weir and his sister off to meet their master, the Devil.

It's hard to understand Weir's sudden confessions and his sister's rapid mental breakdown. Some have suggested that their incestuous relationship was real, and that Weir could not bring himself to believe in his seventieth year that God could forgive him, hence his denouncement and terrible execution. Of course, it could all be true and Weir and his sister were involved in a satanic pact. It is said that towards the end of his life Weir did begin to behave strangely. He would refuse to kneel at prayer and often forgot the words from his Bible, words he had spent decades reading and re-reading. The most damning tale, however, is the one where several people who used to regularly attend his prayer meetings began to refuse to be in his company as they complained that he had begun to exude a strong smell of brimstone…

Further Reading

This is by no means an academic study of witchcraft in Scotland, although the subject does merit serious study. It was a dark time in Scottish (and European) history that accounted for thousands of lives, a time a great turmoil and fear when people from all levels of society were executed for what looks like to us in the 21st century as extremely petty or unsubstantiated accusations.

The best starting point for further study is the Survey of Scottish Witchcraft, carried out by Edinburgh University. It has plenty of resources and links, and comes highly recommended:

http://www.shca.ed.ac.uk/Research/witches/introduction.html

What Witches Do

Alec Beattie

There are, in this town, covens of witches, who by day mutter their curses and concoct their potions, and who by night fly through the air as thickly as autumn-blown leaves. When they are under Satan's spell these witches are hideous to behold and have tempers so fiery they can raise storms and cause mountains to shudder. But when they are not held by dark enchantment such witches appear not unlike any woman known: a wife, a daughter, a mother…such as…

red
haired
Lizzie...

Mistress McDowall, seen digging in the West Kirk cemetery
and then gnawing on the bones of long-dead infants.
The woman, who calls herself Dickson, can talk to beasts
and assume the form of a great, black stallion.
The widow Grant is said to cast no shadow
and to have caused a neighbour's son to become bereft of his wits.
Ill-famed in these parts, the beggarwoman Cowan
inflicts nightmares on those who refuse her charity.
The wife Howie, it is generally understood,
can make those who irk or curse her to disappear without trace.
And the widow Armstrong caused her husband,
much disliked by her, it is well-known, to suddenly fall ill and die.
The daughters of Meg McNulty, no doubt with her guiding hand,
can make young men cast their seed while they sleep.
The milkmaid Geddes, by the utterance of a simple incantation,
can cause a cow's udders to shrivel and dry up.
The crone known as Watt can summon demons and fairies
by offering gifts of good corn bread and the top of the milk.
The wife of the miller at Dalry can cause the crops of neighbours
to become infested with vermin and their beasts to be barren.
The whore, Red-Haired Lizzie, makes clay dolls and suckles them,
so that her spirit can inhabit the bodies of squirrels and foxes.
The fisherwife in Leith known as Matheson can cause
newly landed fish to putrefy before your very eyes.
And the most ungodly of all, the woman Caldwell,
unmarried and childless, who calls herself a Christian,
has within her - and no doubt bestowed upon her
by Beelzebub himself - the power to weaken beer!

Edinburgh's favourite mountain

Sitting with Arthur

Max Scratchmann

Unlike most of the people doing shows in the Fringe, Alec and I actually live in Edinburgh, and the view from the living room of my flat looks straight out onto the majestic Arthur's Seat, which has to be one of the most popular tourist destinations in the city, if the crowds of people crowding onto the summit from dawn to dusk are anything to go by. (Not to mention the folk who flock up there by torch-light on warm summer nights!)

What the brochures don't tell you, however, is that Edinburgh's favourite mountain has a rather sinister history and it's been the site of a lot of grisly deaths over the years. (Though this doesn't appear to worry the hordes of Japanese tourists who write it up on the web with complaints like, "No wi-fi," "No restaurant or toilets at the summit," and, best of all, the man who expressed disappointment that there wasn't a seat provided for him to take a selfie in.)

Much of the mountain's death toll is, of course, from the veritable line of people who regularly plunge to their death from the summit, like the Taiwanese schoolboy who tumbled down headfirst after allegedly posing for a photograph in 2006 – maybe there is a need for a selfie seat after all! – but equally well two erstwhile climbers in the early two-thousands both tumbled down over a hundred feet each in fog on separate occasions and survived, much to the astonishment of ambulance men called out to the scenes.

However, Arthur's Seat boasts some far more sinister deaths from hillside tumbles, where a few unfortunates have had just a little assistance in going headfirst over the summit. The earliest known mountain-top-murderer is a young surgeon called Nicol Muschat, who, in 1719, decided to rid himself of the (rich) simpleton bride he'd just exchanged vows with – literally before the ink was dry on their marriage certificate. Using his, as it turned out to be, imprecise medical knowledge, he first tried to poison the poor lass with mercury, but all he succeeded in doing was putting her through the agonies of the damned but not killing her. And, when she finally recovered, her mental faculties were even more impaired and she clung to him devotedly, telling him daily how grateful she was for his care and attention. Oh the irony.

Undeterred, however, he then went out and hired a bunch of amateur brigands to waylay his simpering wife and murder her, but they were about as useless as he was and bungled the attempt on numerous occasions, each time being surprised by passers-by and running away with the deed half done, so much so that the poor woman was now too afraid to leave the house and spent her waking hours at the window, waiting for Muschat to return home, then clinging to him like glue for the entirety of his evenings at home.

In desperation and fearing for his own sanity by now – you can almost feel sorry for him, can't you? – he resolved to do the deed himself and one fine evening proposed a romantic walk up Arthur's seat in the gloaming, and the wife readily agreed. (It's unlikely that she was seeing much from Muschat in the bedroom department by then and the poor girl must have thought her luck had changed!) They reached the summit just as the sun was setting and – for some inexplicable reason when a simple push would have solved all his problems, he decided to cut her throat instead, weaving some cock-and-bull story to the guards who by then had found his blood-stained scalpel and bloody footprints at the scene, and he was quickly found guilty by the High Court and duly hung in the Grassmarket for his pains.

Sadly, he's only one of the many who have committed capital crimes on Arthur's Seat, and the road leading to the rear of the mountain had already been christened as the Murder Acre by the weavers of Duddingston for almost half a century before Muschat, after an incident there in the summer of 1677 when a dispute over which tradesman's band should play at a march in honour of the king got out of hand. A crowd of about fifteen hundred people had gathered to watch the proposed procession, and it wasn't long before things got ugly and the local magistrates sent out two bailies to instruct the mob to disperse. This show of school-masterly authority made little impression on the Edinburgh rabble, however, and the crowd merely took the bailies hostage, much to the chagrin of the magistrates, who, in a flurry of ruffled feathers, sent out a troop of heavily-armed dragoons to restore order.

Even then things might have been smoothed over with the hostages returned and a few rounds fired over the heads of the mob to satisfy the machismo of the commander, a heavily moustachioed Major Cockburne, but a woman seated on a dyke opposite the Loch – where the car park and the footpath into Duddingston is now – jeered at the troops and accused them of firing blanks. (Literally, what

31

she's reported to have said was: "They've just got powder in their guns, no shot!") This jibe proved to be too much for one soldier in her close vicinity, however, and he fired at her from point-blank range, proving that there was, indeed, lead in his pencil and blew a hole in her middle big enough to "put a fist through".

People were scattering in all directions now, and the one death should have been sufficient to make their point, but Major Cockburne was on a high and ordered his men to open fire into the crowd, and between sixteen and twenty people were gunned down at this popular tourist location by the loch where families flock to feed the ducks each summer.

Fast-wind on a century or two and back up at the summit we find yet another honeymoon killer busily at work. In 1972 a young German couple eloped to Edinburgh and took up residence in a local boarding house where they married – against the wishes of the eighteen-year-old bride's parents – with their landlord and landlady as witnesses.

The couple celebrated their wedding supper at a local restaurant with their patrons, but later, when the household had retired for the night, Herbert Wood, the landlord, was surprised to hear the two newly-weds leaving the building for a midnight stroll on Arthur's Seat "to see the lights". However, he was even more surprised the next morning when he answered the door to an apparently distraught groom and two police officers who informed them that Helga, the teenage bride, had fallen down the mountainside in the dark and was dead.

At this point everyone thought it was just a tragic death, and Dumoulin, the bereaved groom, retreated hastily to the 'honeymoon suite' to be alone, where he was heard playing the theme from Love Story over and over again, and things might have stayed that way had not the landlord decided to clean the room when the police collected the grieving widower to take a routine statement the next morning.

Hidden under a pile of clothing were a string of life insurance policies for a total of over four-hundred-thousand pounds – that's well over a million in today's money – taken out on poor Helga the day before she died, and later enquiries revealed that Dumoulin had shown up at the Princes Street offices of Hambro Life Assurance to try and make a claim on the very morning of the alleged tragedy. (This guy was so subtle!) Even more damning was the revelation that when the company refused to pay out without investigation Dumoulin rescinded his claim and begged them to destroy all the paperwork.

And, as if all this wasn't enough, it was then discovered that back in Germany Dumoulin was a small time crook who had met his teenage bride, a sweet, slightly simple farm girl with no friends, via a loney-hearts advert just three weeks previously and had run away with her in a stolen car – which he then sold to pay the first premium on the insurance policy – and her life savings of sixty-five pounds.

He was tried at the High Court in 1973; where he claimed that Helga, had, in fact, tried to kill him on the mountainside and he had inadvertently pushed her over when he tried to defend himself, but the jury were unconvinced and returned a verdict of guilty after minimal deliberation. He was sentenced to "life" and, having served his time, has since returned to Germany, where, in a suitably fitting punch line to this story, he is now a minister and conducts marriage ceremonies for young eloping couples....

The Baby Farmer

Alec Beattie

In March 1889 Jessie King became the last woman to be hanged in Edinburgh, executed for her part in the murder of two babies. By the time of her death at age twenty seven, King had at least two children of her own and had been paid to adopt three in total. This payment-for-adoption practice, known as 'baby farming' was prevalent in Victorian times when having children out of wedlock was, for women, a threat to an already perilous existence. These unwanted children were more usually the illegitimate offspring of forbidden liaisons between domestic servants or factory workers and their employers, who would be happy to pay the women for their silence and to have the children and any associated shame removed. Despite having to place adverts in something as public as a newspaper, requiring 'parents to adopt a child', the whole affair would be kept as discreet as possible. Most people who paid for such a service would also stipulate that there should be absolutely no further contact with the baby. Jessie King stated she had been paid two pounds to adopt the first of the three babies, little more than a week's wages for a skilled worker.

King was deserted by her father when she was barely a teenager, her mother having died when Jessie was a small child. She moved from orphanage to institution until she was old enough to support herself. Her contemporaries described her as 'being eager to please' but also 'easily duped' and 'melancholic'.

It is likely that King's own pregnancies were the result of prostitution, although she claimed that she was a washerwoman and that the father of her first child deserted her before she gave birth. Her medical records showed that she had been treated for syphilis - typically as a result of prostitution - with mercury, which probably had detrimental effects on her mental health. Just before she gave birth she met and subsequently began to lodge with Thomas Pearson, a man more than twice her age and an alcoholic; Jessie in turn took to drinking herself.

The couple lived in slum properties throughout Edinburgh, Jessie working on the streets of the Old Town, very likely due to pressure from Pearson, when she was able. It is possible that they hit upon the idea of baby farming when Jessie became pregnant and unable to work as a prostitute. In Victorian Edinburgh prostitution and unwanted pregnancies went hand in hand, as well as associated and untreatable diseases such as syphilis. Contraception was virtually non-existent and back-street abortionists were dangerous and ineffectual. It is interesting to note that, alongside newspaper adverts for parents to adopt unwanted babies there ran adverts for such commodities as 'Widow Welch's Pills for Female Complaints', useless and cruel concoctions, sold on the promise that they could resolve 'women's obstructions'.

King strangled or suffocated each of the three children she'd been paid to adopt. If neighbours asked questions about the sudden disappearance of a baby, King and Pearson would move on. It was while they were lodging in Stockbridge that the partially decomposed body of a baby, wrapped in oilskin, was found by children playing, and when the police began their investigations, King and Pearson were arrested.

Pearson quickly turned Queen's evidence, blaming King for all the deaths and claiming he knew nothing. King admitted her guilt and more bodies were discovered. All the while King refused to implicate Pearson in any of the deaths, despite evidence suggesting that, at least, he knew about the children. Pearson walked away while King was found guilty for the deaths of two of the babies she had adopted; the charges for the death of the third child were dropped as a body was never found.

The whole affair and subsequent trial was a scandal that split Edinburgh society. A group of well-to-do women campaigned on King's behalf, petitioning for clemency and ensuring that references to the 'influences of another' made the newspapers while others vilified her, likening her to a 'cornered rat' and demanding that members of the public be allowed to witness her on the gallows.

While awaiting her execution King was examined by several medical practitioners who concluded she was sane and 'fit to hang'. Objections were raised and some witnesses at her trial reported that she appeared 'melancholic' and that her demeanour suggested she was 'hauf jackit' a pejorative term for someone with learning disabilities.

Needless to say, justice took its course. In her final days King became overly-religious, spending long periods in her cell praying. The High Court prohibited witnesses from attending the execution (members of the press were usually allowed to observe executions). The hangman, James Berry, reported that King was calm, and that her last words were, 'Oh, to be hanged! What a death!'

Pearson didn't escape justice entirely; exactly a year and a day after Jessie King's execution he was found dead, a fatal wound on the back of his head…

But the gallows holds me high...

The Ballad of Jessie King

Alec Beattie

They cry me Jessie King and I'm tae be hingit in the morn
For fellin bairns and childer, the swaddellin and newborn
I tak the mammies' sins and dochters a' for a haun o' siller
They didnae ken, not ain o' them, that I'm a cauld-hertit killer

A washerwife sin I was yon tae mak a sma o' breid
Fan I was boukit wi a' limmerin I wushed that I was deid
But canny Pearson tak me in an I thocht that he was couthie
But time soon telt he was no mair than a hackit-faced auld drouthie

But man I was forespoken e'en though he'd gowff me sore
An' mak me drink his mockit craitur and roup me for a hoor
An fan I was creesh and bound and nae guid to man nor beast
He bid me become a fermer o' weans, to bring a dram tae the feast

An' so I tak the wean's o' folk who dinna want them for their ain
I tak the luve bairns for sma bawbies an bring the wee gets hame
An fan I canna tak ony mair o their greetin an their mess
I thrapple them wi my bare hauns and hod them in the press

I fell my ain an a' ye see, a' shilpit wi nae faither
An he hunkered there and leuked ower me like it was nae baither
Ne'er yince did he try and stap me frae' my frichtsome ack
An when the polis came hinmaist he stug us in the back

He cliped on me to save his scruff and his neck frae the noose:
"I ne'er kenned aboot the bairns she hod in oor peerie hoose
Ne'er harkened a whimper or a yout or tak a noxious smell
It wisnae me the sleekit ratton did them in hersel'"

I didna argie. I kenned my crime an kenned my tid was run
I speired my jilers for a Bible and said guid words tae God the Son
Tae tak my sowel intae his hert and forgive me a' my sins
An tak up a' the bairns an weans an a' the ither yins

And now I bide hereaboots as the daylicht fills the jile
The widdie bides ootside for me, we'll forgaither in a while
I howp it disna skaith ower much when the hangie taks my neck
But the widdie hauds me heich an my speerit disna brek

The Ballad of Jessie King

translation by Alec Beattie

If you're not fortunate enough to speak or understand Scots, the following is a translation into plain English. Sadly, it loses a lot of its original lyricism and natural rhythm...

They call me Jessie King and I'm to be hanged in the morn
For killing babes and children, the swaddling and newborn
I took the mothers' sons and daughters all for a hand of silver
They didn't know, not one of them, that I'm a cold-hearted killer

A washerwoman since I was young to make a little bread
When I fell pregnant through whoring I wished that I was dead
One smart Pearson took me in and I thought that he was clever
But time soon told he was no more than an ugly drunkard

But man, I was bewitched even though he sorely hit me
And made me drink his horrible whisky and sold me for a whore
And when I was fat and pregnant and no good to man nor beast
He made me become a child farmer, to bring whisky to our table

I took the children of others who didn't want them for their own
I took the bastards for little money and took the mongrels home
And when I couldn't take any more of their crying or their mess
I strangled them with my bare hands and hid them in the press

I killed my own as well you see, all dirty with no father
And he sat there and looked me over like it was no bother
Not once did he try to stop me from my frightening deeds
And when the police finally came he stabbed me in the back

He told on me to save his skin and his neck from the noose:
"I never knew about the children she hid in our little house
Never heard a whimper nor a scream nor smelt a noxious stink
It wasn't me the crafty rat killed them all by herself"

I didn't argue. I knew my crime and knew my time had run out
I asked my jailers for a Bible and prayed to God the Son
To take my soul into His heart and forgive me all my sins
And take up all the children and babes and all the other ones

And now I wait here awhile as daylight fills the jail
The gallows waits outside for me; we'll meet up in a while
I hope it doesn't hurt too much when the hangman takes my neck
But the gallows holds me high and my spirit doesn't break

The Doctor's Dilemma

Max Scratchmann

At best it's a black comedy, at worst a grisly murder the like of which True Detective would probably have headlined *Stoned Doctor Slays Pregnant Parent*, but, surprisingly, this is not a bloody tale of drug-fuelled slaughter from the dark and seedy back alleys of the Grassmarket but instead a gratuitous fest of gore and gloop from the sedate terraces of Joppa just along the prom from sleepy Portobello.

Our story starts in February 1914 when Jane Anderson, a policeman's wife, went into labour with her first child and called out the local doctor, Hugh Dewar, a well-liked and well-respected Portobello medic. It's hard to get an accurate picture of Dewar, as his popularity with the ladies of Portobello has eroded the facts in the case, but we do know that he was forty-eight at the time of the incident, had been practicing medicine for eighteen years and was unmarried and lived in Portobello with his spinster sisters.

Maybe that was why he was so popular with the Joppa womenfolk? Or was it, maybe, his Shipman-like charm and cosy bedside manner that made him such a sugar daddy? Who knows! What we do know is that when Jane Anderson went into painful labour she had no hesitation in sending for Dewar, and, despite the lateness of the hour, it wasn't long before he was propping his bike up in front of the

skilful physician

Anderson residence and rolling up his shirtsleeves to get down to the serious business of birthing the child.

Now, this wasn't Dewar's first birth, by any means, and he'd scorned the assistance of a midwife and was in the room with only the – by now – contracting Jane and her mother, Mrs McArthur, who noticed that the medic was off his game quite early in the proceedings.

"I drew his attention to things like a saturated binder – that's a long white swaddling cloth tide round the stomach to keep the mother's abdominal muscles supported – but he appeared not to notice," she later told an inquest. "In fact, it's like he wasn't really there…"

Then to make matters worse, the birth was proving difficult and the mother was in considerable discomfort by now – though it was small potatoes to what she was about to suffer at the hands of Doctor Death – and so Dewar resorted to using forceps. Rather badly, as it happened.

We now know that he punctured the posterior wall of Jane Anderson's vagina, producing an acute retrovaginal fistula "large enough to admit the introduction of a hand". He'd also torn the wall of the caecum and Jane's intestinal lining was – cover your ears if you're squeamish – literally hanging out of her vagina.

Time to call out an ambulance or at least call for help, you'd think, but Dewar's actual words were: "Here is something that should not be here" and he proceeded not to make reparation but to try and pull the offending item out of her body.

Now, I can only begin to imagine the pain that that poor girl was suffering right then, having first given birth and then having to further endure the bungling ineptitude of the muddled medic who was presiding over her, and it's a pity that police constable Anderson, the proud father who was no doubt pacing behind the closed door, didn't burst into the room and punch Dewar in the nose.

As it happens, though, no-one intervened, even the girl's mother, while Dewar proceeded to pull out over fifteen feet of Jane's large intestinal lining, stretching from the caecum to the rectum.

Try and imagine that with me. One foot, 2, 3, 4, 5, 6, 7, 8, 9, 10, 11, 12, 13, 14, 15. Now, I'm not a doctor and I've never been in a delivery room, but, come on, even I would be thinking something was wrong by the time I'd got to about two feet. Wouldn't you?

Not our Hughie, however, and he just dumped the offending – well, I'm not sure what he would have called it – 'stuff' into a chamber pot and went off on his way, content that he'd delivered a "healthy wee boy" and left Jane Anderson to die a horrible death, three long hours later. "In much agony" as a wry medical examiner inadequately described it in the subsequent "necropsy".

History gets muddy round about now, but the reigning medical examiner finally deemed that the case was one of culpable homicide and – er – three weeks later a couple of policemen picked up Dewar and charged him, though they then promptly let him out on bail and he continued to practice while awaiting trial and a simultaneous private lawsuit for malpractice until he was found dead from a overdose a week before his trial.

Oddly enough, in the rush to bury Dewar, they didn't get round to doing an autopsy, despite his erratic behaviour and even though the police found unspecified "poison" on his person at the time of his arrest, so whatever Dewar's personal narcotic habits they've long since been whitewashed away.

The local community and Dewar's angry patients, though, they would have seen through all this medical cover-up, wouldn't they, and gone out with their pitchforks to burn down Dr Death's surgery and eradicate all trace of him and his murderous ineptitude? Wouldn't they?

Nope, they went out and raised three hundred and ten pounds, seven shillings and four-pence and built a monument to him, "a skilful and beloved physician... lost in the prime of manhood!" It's still there today in Abercorn Park, just a few minutes from the sea.

You should go visit...

There's Been A Murder!

Alec Beattie

George Meikle Kemp was born the son of a shepherd and, when old enough, apprenticed to a carpenter. He ran away, age 15, to study the architecture of the great cities of Europe and became a self-taught draughtsman and architect.

On his return to Edinburgh he could not find employment as an architect because he had not received any formal education or training, and was working class at a time when a man (women of any strata in society were not allowed a university education) had to be from the professional, educated middle classes to become an architect. This was compounded by Kemp's mental state; it is very likely he suffered from a bipolar disorder. It is well-documented by his friends and contemporaries that he suffered from depression – what they described as 'melancholia'. When George became manic he suffered from delusional behaviour and would claim that God drew designs in the sky for him to copy, leading to his rivals labelling him 'the mad carpenter'. Despite bouts of illness Kemp made a good living as an accomplished joiner and draughtsman, married, and began to raise a family.

In 1832 the people of Edinburgh began to gather subscriptions to pay for a monument to Sir Walter Scott, with a competition and a fifty guinea prize for the winning design. Kemp entered under an assumed name and won. However, when his identity was discovered, his competitors were outraged, taking notices out in Edinburgh newspapers claiming that Kemp, the 'mad carpenter' was unfit to design the monument.

Kemp never saw his design realised. One foggy evening in March 1844, halfway through the building of the monument, Kemp disappeared. His body was discovered almost a week later in the Union canal, at the Lochrin basin in Fountainbridge where the stone for the monument was unloaded from canal barges.

What happened next is what nowadays would be described as a 'cold case', a death or disappearance that remains unexplained…until now.

When Kemp's body was found the Edinburgh Mob took to the streets to protest. Kemp was a working man, one of their own and popular about the town; the Mob smelled a rat.

A story was quickly printed in Edinburgh newspapers, fuelled and paid for by Kemp's competitors who were fearful of reprisals: 'Kemp had got lost in a dense fog the night he disappeared, and had fallen into the canal and drowned.'

But the Edinburgh Mob cried: No! We will not be duped! Kemp walked the path from the construction site on Princes Street, through the Fountainbridge canal basin, and on to his house in Morningside four times a day for two years. He knew the path like the back of his hand, and anyway, the Mob reasoned, how thick must the fog have been for Kemp to have fallen into the canal! They didn't accept this reasoning and continued their noisy protest.

The newspapers quickly printed another story: 'Kemp had got drunk and fallen, insensible, into the canal and drowned.'

Again the Mob would not be fooled, and Kemp's

friends and colleagues took out notices in the newspapers themselves. 'You should not speak ill of the dead,' the notice began, going on to say that George was a man of temperate habits who drank no more nor less than any other man. One enterprising sleuth visited all the places along Kemp's path that sold alcohol – inns, taverns and hotels – and not one person saw Kemp the night he disappeared, let alone having sold him a drop of alcohol.

The newspapers quickly printed a third story: 'Kemp, as we all know, was a melancholy man. It is not beyond belief that, in a fit of despair, he took his own life.'

Once more, the Edinburgh Mob would not be duped. On the day he disappeared Kemp had written in his diary that working on the Scott monument was 'work to be greatly cherished'. His son then disclosed that, in the week before his death, Kemp had apprenticed him to work beside him, remarking that it was 'his life's greatest joy.' With this knowledge Kemp's followers reasoned that this was not the behaviour of a man contemplating suicide, and they dismissed this third explanation.

The newspapers then printed a fourth scenario: 'Kemp, walking home through the fog, was attacked and robbed then his body thrown into the canal.'

However, when the circumstances of the discovery of Kemp's body were revealed, the Edinburgh Mob once again took to the streets. Kemp's body had been found when his hat had floated to the surface of the canal. The fashion at the time was for a gentleman to attach his hat to his belt using a piece of string so if it was blown off, it could be recovered; Kemp's hat was still attached to his belt. When his body was recovered he also had his silk gloves and his purse with the money inside. What kind of robber, the

Mob argued, would fail to take a man's valuables? He was not robbed at all!

Kemp's enemies knew they were on a hiding to nothing so they did one final thing: they kept their peace. And, although the death of Kemp provoked ill-feeling for months to come, the passage of time lessened the Mob's anger, and the story of George Meikle Kemp faded into memory. Indeed, it has faded so much that there is little known about the mysterious events surrounding his death.

However, there's one more possible explanation for Kemp's death, one that wasn't suggested at the time or any time since. Until now; we've a fifth explanation, and we're so sure of it that we're willing to put it up against these four suggestions, and think on this: do an online search and the accepted version is still that Kemp got lost in the fog and fell into the canal.

Point one: Kemp's friends reported that, before he died, Kemp was 'in fair health and humour' and that he was a 'tenacious swimmer'. Even if Kemp had fallen into the canal in the fog, it seems he would have had a fair chance of saving himself, or, at least, calling for help.

Two: Kemp's body lay at the bottom of the Lochrin basin for a week. When it was discovered, thanks to his hat, it was found to have been weighed down; stone meant for the monument was found on and about the body. After much experimentation we've discovered that to in order to submerge and weigh down a body in water it has to be immobile; that is, unconscious or dead; live people tend to struggle. It could be argued that someone had deliberately tried to conceal Kemp's body.

Three: there were no witnesses. Despite the night of Kemp's disappearance being unusually foggy, the Lochrin basin was a busy place of work. The transportation of goods via canal was slow and expensive and barge companies made the most of available time and workers. There was a continuous stream of canal traffic going through the Lochrin basin, particularly because of the stone needed for the Scott monument. And One of Kemp's contractors called Lind kept offices and watchmen at the Lochrin basin, to stop thieving. But no-one saw reported that they saw or heard anything suspicious that night. Again, it could be argued that someone deliberately – and surreptitiously – concealed the body.

Finally, point four: the job of completing the half-finished monument went to a consortium of Kemp's rivals, men and architects who had opposed him in life and defamed him in death. They made a small fortune on the well-funded monument project.

It seems unlikely that Kemp ended up in the Lochrin basin because he became lost in the fog or through inebriation or despair. If he was robbed why didn't the robbers take his valuables before throwing his body into the canal?

The more accepted versions of Kemp's demise pale when you consider these further details: he was healthy and strong and by all accounts could swim well. His body appears to have been deliberately concealed and there were no witnesses on the night he supposedly disappeared. Finally, his competitors gained financially at least from his death.

What's it to be? Lost in the fog? Fell into the canal drunk? Threw himself to a watery end? Robbed and his body disposed of in the canal? Or is it more likely that Kemp was murdered by rivals and his body deliberately concealed?

You decide...

The Mad Carpenter

Alec Beattie

Born with the blood of shepherds in your veins
you were destined to work wood with your hands.
Instead you wandered in foreign cities,
sought out the building blocks of construction.

And you thought you were Christ from Judea,
your father drawing time pieces for you
in the sky, clocks that set out a future
where you would dream up your edifices.

Ashamed of your low birth, lack of station,
outsider. Or afraid to let them see
your light, your design that led to Heaven,
You concealed yourself behind John Morvo.

And still, you, the Mad Carpenter, won through.
Your craft was chosen, a monumental
tribute for some but for you a skywards
beacon to guide the lost back to the path.

And then you were lost before your design
was realised. A mysterious
death left unresolved, the jigsaw puzzle
with one vital piece forever missing.

Really Dead Certain

Max Scratchmann

It's unlikely that many visitors to the city will include a visit to Lochend Park in Restalrig on their itinerary, and, at first glance, it would seem to be easy to see why. After all, there's not much to see. There's the Loch, of course, though it's in reality little more than an elevated duck pond, with no swirling river or miniature waterfall to fill it, and it seems that the "bottomless" lake is fed behind the scenes by several underground springs. Blocks of modern flats look down disdainfully across the park's rather lumpy grass on one side, a sprawling low rise post-war council estate hugs its borders on the other. A typical suburban green space, then, and not special enough to boast a guide book entry or the interest of historians.

Yet a huge medieval doocott sits in the shadow of the steep rock face at the east shore of the water, hinting that maybe something grand had stood here back in the day; and take a closer look at the foundations of the unexceptional nineteenth-century Lochend House and you'll spot what looks to be a fireplace and a window lintel - in fact, all that's left of the once impressive Lochend Castle, a place of great wealth and power. And, you'll be pleased to know, a fair amount of intrigue, murder and general skullduggery to boot.

The vast lands of Restalrig and Craigentinny within the city - plus further lands in Ayrshire and the Borders

- were all the property of the extremely powerful Logan family who had laid claim to the Barony of Restalrig in the fourteenth century and taken up residence in the castle by the loch soon after. Accounts vary as to their temperament and ability to rule, but the estate continued to flourish and grow until the mid-sixteenth century when the young Sir Robert Logan inherited the estate, along with other parcels of land and Fast Castle in the Borders from his mother's second husband.

Now, whereas Logan senior was said to be an able and temperate laird, the young Sir Robert was well know for his profligate lifestyle of drinking, gambling and whoring and was described in one contemporary account as "a godless, drunkin' and deboshit man". Several parts of the huge estate were sold off during his lifetime to cover his many debts, and when he finally died of his excesses in 1606 the lands and fortunes of the family were much diminished.

No matter. Sir Robert's widow still had the castle and modest rents to keep her solvent and, it seemed, all would be well for the troubled family now that the drunken spendthrift was safely out of the way and entombed in the family vaults of nearby South Leith parish church. Unfortunately for the widow Logan, however, trouble of a different sort was brewing elsewhere in Scotland and was about to impact on her in a way in which no-one could have envisaged.

A band of conspirators led by John Ruthann, the Third Earl of Gowrie, had been meeting in secret to unfold an - unsuccessful - plot to murder James IV (he of the King James Bible fame) and the principal "Gowrie Conspirators" - Ruthann and his brother, Alexander, the master of Ruthven, were executed at Perth and bodies brought to Edinburgh and put on display. End of story, you might think, but greedy eyes were focusing on the castle at Lochend and the heirless widow in residence.

Ruthann and his brother had been condemned on the testimony of one George Sprot of Eyemouth - obtained under torture, of course - and in 1608, Sprot, who was still incarcerated and hoping, no doubt, to save his own neck, added further names to his existing list of malefactors and named Sir Robert Logan of Restalrig as another Gowrie conspirator on the strength of a single letter to the Earl he had caught sight of, allegedly signed "Restalrig". (Needless to say, the said letter was never produced in evidence.)

Unluckily for Sprot, this revelation didn't prove sufficient testimony to absolve him of his sins, and he was duly hanged at the Grassmarket in August of 1608 for "having prior knowledge of the conspiracy". And again, you'd think this was the end of the story, but despite Logan's alleged part in the conspiracy being considered "a mere invention of [Sprot's] own brain" it didn't stop the authorities of the day levelling a charge of high treason against him, and his corpse was exhumed and brought to the High Court to stand trial.

Amazingly, the deceased defendant entered no plea when stood in the dock, so the trial went ahead, and one Alexander Watson, the Kirk Minister of Coldingham, where the Logan family just so happened to have estates, testified to having seen the letter in question and swore that "the spelling and hand of the missive" was that of Robert Logan, leaving the court no option but find him guilty of high treason, send his corpse to be hanged and - surprise, surprise - forfeit his lands, throwing his widow and surviving daughter into abject poverty.

The Mouse Who Saved Edinburgh Castle

Alec Beattie

Edinburgh in the Shadows isn't all about death, drugs, disaster, murder, burning and throttling...Okay, it's mostly about death, drugs, disaster and all that but there's also a little space to feature a relatively unknown hero in the town's history. One for the bairns too, so sit back, put your baffies on and settle down to enjoy the following tale of a rather valiant rodent...

SNAP!

'Come gather ye round and hear telt the tale o' the mousie who saved Edinburgh Castle and all the souls therein from the invading English armies...'

'Twas when the English King Henry - the yin who liked to cut aff the heids o' his wives - greatly coveted the Scottish crown; he wanted it all for himself. Oor ain Queen Mary was herself but a bairn so the Scots Lairds, in her place, telt auld Henry to keep his hands tae himself. Henry was fair affronted. He took great offense at no' getting what he saw as his kingly right so he sent a huge army up north tae punish Scotland, putting town and village tae sword and flame in their wake. It was a rough wooing indeed, if there ever was yin.

When Henry's army reached the castle o' old Edinburgh toon they laid siege. The might o' the English artillery, using their huge war machines and cannon, muskets and ranks o' archers, found that nae matter what they tried they couldnae find a way tae break the castle's thick, strong walls or the spirit o' the garrison that protected them. Weeks became months while the English army used up their gunpowder and missiles. Their food began tae fester and run oot and their soldiers and livestock began to fall ill while the castle remained untaken. They tried tae find and bribe spies but tae nae avail; not yin person in the toon would accept a traitor's payment of silver.

Yin day in late summer, as the rain fell in sheets and the wind whipped the wind from the north, the English generals argued in the grand tent that served as their headquarters and decided tae pack up and go home. Better tae face the anger o' the now-defeated King Henry than tae stay encamped ootside Edinburgh castle, wi' disease and hunger killing more English soldiers than any Scottish yin had managed, and wi' the cruel Scottish winter on its way.

Just then twin brothers wi' identical greasy black hair, rotten teeth, and ragged clothes presented themselves tae the generals.

"My Lords," yin o' them said with a flourish, "for months my brother and I have been watching and studying the castle closely."

"Very closely," his brother echoed.

"We know how to scale the rock," he continued, " and a way inside through an unguarded drain. We wait until the garrison's asleep, climb inside and open the gate. All you need to do is march in your soldiers."

The eldest of the generals eyed the brothers. "And what do you request, by way of reward, if you can do what you claim?"

"We came north with your army to seek our fortune. We ask that we be given land and titles, here, in Scotland, so that we may lord it over these Scottish peasants!"

Some o' the generals laughed while others argued. But when they reached the consensus that they had nothing tae lose by letting the twins find a way inside the castle, they agreed tae let them try.

"I do not know which is worse," one of the generals said tae the twins. "Scaling that rock in the dark, or wanting to remain in this terrible country."

When the dark o' the night had shrouded the castle the brothers set off. Swift and silent they began tae scale the rock, moving towards the unguarded drain where unseen they slipped inside. Both carried clubs in case they had tae silence any guard they encountered but they were so stealthy they made their way through the castle undetected as if they were mere shadows.

Now, at the same time a mouse was sniffing about looking for its dinner when its keen ears heard the low murmurs of unfamiliar accents - the two intruders, in their excitement, were foolishly whispering and boasting tae yin another o' the riches tae come. The mouse knew everyone inside the castle; in its quest for food it had gotten tae know who would drop the odd crumb or other morsel but these voices were not known tae him. The mouse scurried off towards the noise and when it saw the two brothers it immediately knew that they were up tae nae good. The mouse followed them, thinking on how he could alert the sleeping guards.

But, the mouse knew, his tiny squeak would never be able tae wake a sleeping guard! He had tae think of something quickly before the two intruders began whatever loathsome task they were there tae carry out.

The pair stole intae the guardhouse, crept up behind the dozing guards, and knocked them oot with a quick blow from their clubs. From the shadows the mouse appeared and crept up tae yin o' the guards lying on the floor. It had to try and rouse him, so it stuck its muzzle in the guard's ear and shrieked a squeak tae wake the deid, but tae nae avail. The guard merely snored.

Taking the keys the twins unlocked the gatehouse wherein the machinery that drove the locks and bars that held the castle's gate shut lay. The mouse followed them and saw his chance! High above the intruders hung a huge wooden chandelier, lit by twenty four candles, tae light up the windowless gatehouse. The mouse then knew if he could chew his way through the rope that held the chandelier it would fall on them before the two rogues could work the heavy lock that held the gate shut! The race was on!

The mouse was clever, for he began tae chew through the rope where years o' lowering and raising the chandelier had worn it. Behind him the brothers worked slowly, turning the huge wheel that moved the iron bar holding the gates closed. But, the mouse saw, they were slowing. The work o' turning the wheel was tiring them.

The mouse chewed and chewed. His jaws were beginning tae ache and burn with pain but when he saw the intruders were near tae opening the gates he steeled himself and chewed with all his might. But the brothers in their turn had gotten their second wind and were working harder than ever, and the poor mouse still had much rope tae chew through. Then he had an idea; he saw a tin cup sitting at the edge o' a nearby table. If he could push the cup on tae the floor the noise might distract them long enough...

The mouse scampered along the table top and crashed intae the cup, sending it clattering and clanging on the floor. It had worked! When they heard the noise the pair froze. Their hands moved slowly tae their clubs, ready tae fight off whoever had disturbed them. But the mouse took nae heed o' them. It ran back tae the rope and began once again to chew furiously.

"To work, brother," one o' the twins said, looking about the guardhouse. "There's no-one here. It must have been the wind." Then, wi' a grunt, the two men again began tae work on the wheel that held the gate closed.

The mouse felt his heart race and hammer in his chest. He began tae believe he would fail when he heard the rope creak and strain under the weight of the chandelier. He saw that the bar was about to clear the door and he closed his eyes, ready tae offer up a prayer, when SNAP!

The rope finally broke and the chandelier crashed doon on the unsuspecting brothers, crushing them and holding fast the gates.

The noise brought guards who seized the two intruders and locked the gates again; ootside the English soldiers, when they heard the commotion inside the castle, knew that all was lost. They slunk away and prepared tae march home.

Some said it was Providence that caused the rope tae snap, squash the intruders, and save the castle. But yin guard had held the broken end of the rope in his hand and saw that it had been chewed through. He thanked whatever sharp-brained and sharp-toothed beastie who had saved them.

And so, from that night on the brave mouse who had saved Edinburgh castle dined on the finest bread and cheese, left out for him by the grateful guard.

There ye have it, my friends. And bear in mind now, tae put your faith in the smallest o' things, like the wee mousie who saved the castle. Never a truer tale was telt.'

Resurrection Men

Max Scratchmann

No book on the dark side of Edinburgh would be complete without at least a nod to the original resurrection men, the infamous Burke and Hare, a pair of notorious ne'er-do-wells who supplied cadavers to the burgeoning Edinburgh medical schools. At first they just sold the bodies of the poor, then they turned to grave robbing, and, finally, to murder, clocking up a grand total of sixteen corpses before they were finally apprehended.

In the midnight fog they loom large, the taste of them sulphurous on the tongue,
Like the blunt blade of an old lead spade.

Watch out for the winking yellow eye of their sleepy lanterns,
Watch out for the frosty kiss of their laboured breath on your icy window pane,
The graveyards have given up their dead, but still this pair hunger.

Two tall-hatted creatures of the smoky Edinburgh night,
Outdoing any limp English Boogie Man that Ealing Studios could dream up,
Nah, these two are the real McCoy,
Made in Scotland from girders,
In the premier league of deep-fried Mars Bars and Hi Pizza Pie,
Uniquely Scottish, and without even a hint of tartan,
Obsidian comedians of the dark who'll slit your throat for a shilling and then buy you a drink with the change.

Butch & Sundance, Fred & Rosemary, Myra & Ian,
Synonymous names irrevocably linked with a deadly ampersand,
Canongate Doxies, Fleshmarket Foxies or Fingzies Poxies,
Dive bar harlots of Henry Jeckyll's alter ego and the habitués

of the fog-banked haunts of….
Burke & Hare.
Nah, no trite tourist-trap ghost bus here!

So,
Come – visit – if – you – dare.
Edinburgh.
City of bones.

About the Authors

Alec Beattie is a writer, promoter and performer. He's been involved in the Edinburgh spoken word scene for years and currently runs and co-hosts Blind Poetics. As well as being an Edinburgh Fringe regular he's performed his poetry and short stories throughout Scotland. His third novel is due for publication in September 2016, and he's also published a collection of short stories, details of which can be found at www.alecbeattie.org. He lives in Edinburgh with his partner and two cats.

Max Scratchmann is one half of the Poetry Circus as well as being an illustrator, writer and performer, equally well known for his dark art and black comedy. He is a regular at the Edinburgh Fringe and was one of the four Inky Fingers' Poets on a Bus at the Edinburgh History Festival. He lives in Edinburgh in a depressingly cat-free household.

Gracia Navas is a self-taught artist and illustrator and works as a professional freelance translator. She did the illustrations for several stories published in the Duality books series between 2010 and 2013. In 2014, one of her drawings was selected for the Royal Scottish Academy Open Exhibition. When she is not working or drawing, she loves reading, gardening and watching her cats. She lives in Edinburgh with her partner.

About the Show

Want to know the Edinburgh the tourist guides won't tell you about? Beattie and Scratchmann tell it like it really is in this spoken word show about the city's sinister side with stories, tales and poems of drugs and murder, witchcraft and fetishes, executions and hauntings, cover ups and botch jobs that reveal the truth behind Edinburgh's lesser-known miscreants, unfortunates and flawed geniuses.

Edinburgh in the Shadows – stories the tourist guides never reveal...

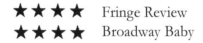 Fringe Review
★ ★ ★ ★   Broadway Baby

'thoroughly dark and entertaining'
'kept the audience amused, aghast and attentive'
'darkly fascinating historical laughs and thrills'
'grimly amusing'

First performed in June 2015, Edinburgh in the Shadows has entertained and amused audiences at the Celtic Mystery Festival, the Grassmarket Festival, the Merchant City Comedy Festival, and the Edinburgh Fringe Festival. It's also sold out at the National Library of Scotland, and toured libraries, cafes, pubs and clubs throughout Edinburgh. Back on the road for 2016, the show will be performed at the Cowgatehead venue during the Edinburgh Fringe Festival, with a warm up tour of Edinburgh's finest reading establishments.

Follow Us

Sheboygan, **GROH & BRO.,** Wisconsin.

www.alecbeattie.org
www.blindpoetics.wordpress.com
www.facebook.com/alec.beattie1
www.twitter.com/alec_beattie
www.amazon.co.uk/-/e/B016UXWN0K

Sheboygan, GROH & BRO., Wisconsin.

maxscratchmann.com
comicpoems.wordpress.com
freakcircus.co.uk
poetrycircus.co.uk
Amazon Author Page:
tinyurl.com/z7rfzdy

www.edinburghintheshadows.wordpress.com
www.facebook.com/Edinburgh-in-the-Shadows-2-883873105071506
www.twitter.com/EintheS

Printed in Great Britain
by Amazon